Adults

Easiest
Beginner
Piano Method

Gordon Banks Piano Method
"We keep it simple"

This book is for those of us who suffer from 'less'.
Less time, less opportunity, less attention span,
Less memory, less talent, less finger dexterity…,
yet still have the desire to play a keyboard or piano.
Learning to play to whatever degree can occupy our
leisure time creatively and prove to be a most
interesting and ever expanding hobby.

On Youtube: Gordon Banks Piano Method

Copyright 2015 by Gordon Banks,
Jennings-Lane Publishing
239-272-0336   Naples, Florida

Contents

Your Keyboard

The keyboard has black keys and white keys. In this book we will be using only the white keys.

The white keys follow the alphabet from A to G, going left to right. There is no H, I, J, K ; just A to G repeating over and over, like a stairway going from floor to floor, higher and higher.

Since all the white keys look alike we identify them by looking at the groups of black keys. THE BLACK KEYS ARE IN GROUPS OF EITHER TWO OR THREE KEYS. The most important key, the C key is <u>always</u> the white key immediately to the left of each group of TWO black keys. See the photo below.

Your 10 fingers will use only 5 white keys. Your right hand will use the group of C,D,E,F,G closest to the center of your keyboard. Your left hand will use the next group of C,D,E,F,G to the left of your right hand group. Let's turn the page.

5 Fingers / 5 Keys

The C key is always the white key immediately to the left
of the groups of two (2) black keys.

See the picture below. Place your right hand thumb on the C key
nearest the middle of your keyboard. Your remaining four fingers
on D,E,F,G.
Next find the C key to the left of your right hand thumb. This is just
7 white keys to the left. Place your left hand 'pinky' on that C key
and the remaining 4 fingers on D,E,F,G. Rest all ten fingers on
those keys. Use this hand position for all songs in this book.

The Right Hand note values

What does the right hand do?
    The right hand plays the part we recognize,
    the melody.

How do we read sheet music?
    We read **notes**. Notes tell us which keys to push down
    and how much time the key stays down while we count
    to four.

We need to count?
    Yes, like marching: 1,2,3,4,1,2,3,4. A song is
    recognized by which keys are played and how long
    each is held down. Counting allows us to be very
    precise in the length of time a key is held down.

Look below. These are the **NOTES** you will be using.
    1. Notes are circles, plus extras.
    2. Notes alone, like those below tell us how long to
       hold down a key, **while we are counting**.

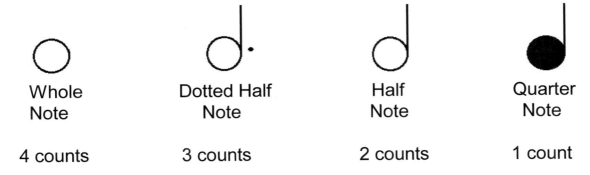

Whole Note	Dotted Half Note	Half Note	Quarter Note
4 counts	3 counts	2 counts	1 count

For example: A whole note is worth 4 counts. This means your key is
pressed down on count 1 and is held down through counts 2,3,4, then
released. Counting is done at a steady pace like counting steps while
marching. Your goal is to be counting without frequent stops and starts.

Questions? See tutorials on Youtube: Gordon Banks Piano Method.

Counting Notes

So here we are counting to four, over and over. Hold down the whole note while counting to four (1,2,3,4). A quarter note gets just one count. Below is a whole note worth a count of 1,2,3,4. Then 4 quarter notes (each worth 1 count) and another whole note worth a count of 1,2,3,4. **Pick a key, any key** and play the pattern below while counting.

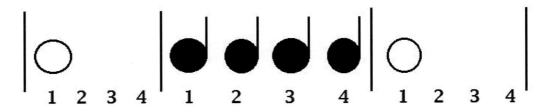

Each group of notes equaled a count of 1,2,3,4.

Each four count group is placed in a box called a **measure**. The same exercise as above now looks like this group below when placed into measures.

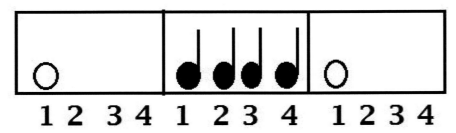

Pick a key and play this group again, while counting.

Play these three measures below while counting 1,2,3,4. The half notes receive two counts and a quarter note receives one count. Each measure totals 4 counts when its note values are added up.

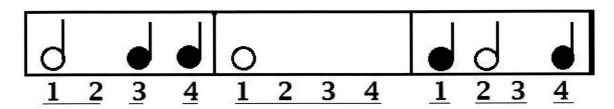

Right Hand Measure

Notes are placed in a box called a **measure**. We have seen what
a whole note, a dotted half note, half note and quarter note look like:

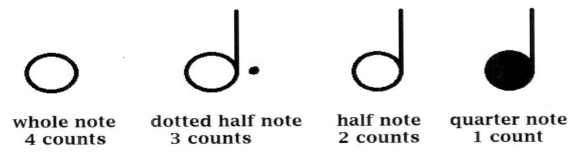

whole note	dotted half note	half note	quarter note
4 counts	3 counts	2 counts	1 count

Each box is made up of 5 horizontal lines and 4 spaces. Each line and
each space represents a specific key near the middle of the keyboard.
The note's circle is placed in a space or directly over a line passing
through its center. A different line or space for each key.
Like the keyboard, these lines and spaces also go up the alphabet to G,
then start over. **We will use 5 keys: middle C and D,E,F,G.**

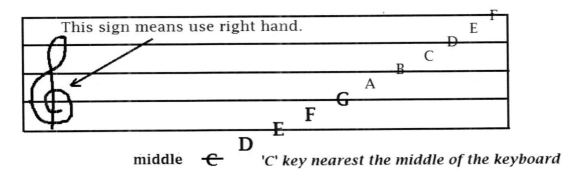

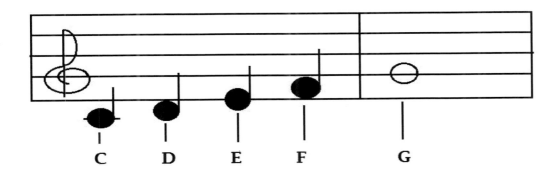

Right Hand: 5 fingers, 5 keys

In this book your right hand uses 5 keys: C,D,E,F,G. One for each finger.
Your right hand thumb is finger number 1, then fingers 2,3,4,5.
Remember, the C key is always the white key to the left of each group
of **two** black keys. Find the C key nearest the middle of your keyboard.
Middle C, is the new home for your thumb. Starting with your thumb on
middle C, place your five fingers on C,D,E,F,G. Play the exercises below.
It is important to count 1,2,3,4 out loud while getting used to counting.
At first your counting might start and stop, start and stop while
looking for your specific keys. Work towards a steady count.

These are whole notes, worth 4 counts each.

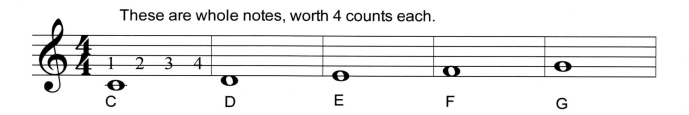

These are half notes, worth 2 counts each: 1 half note + 1 half note = 4 counts.

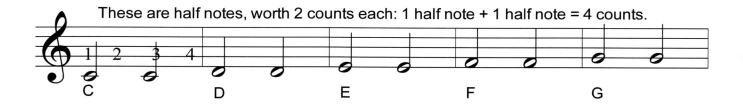

These are quarter notes, worth 1 count each: 1 + 1 + 1 + 1 = 4 counts.

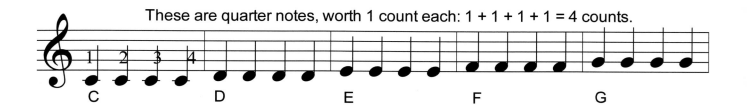

Notes with different counts can be placed in the same measure.
Together they must equal 4 counts.

More About Counting and Playing

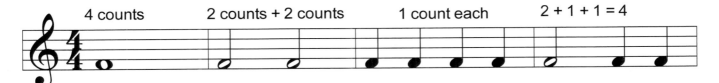

A line of measures in a row is called a **staff**.

This sign: **4/4** one 4 over another 4 (seen above in the first measure) means each measure of the staff contains four counts.

Below is another **right hand exercise**. Find middle C. Place your right hand fingers on keys C,D,E,F,G. This is called the **C position**.

Hold down each key for the number of counts listed above each measure. Remember, each measure counts 1,2,3,4.

First Melody: counting

This is a counting exercise for the song First Melody. This song will
be played on the following page. First read the instructions below.

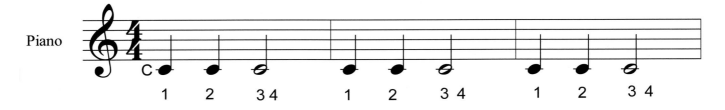

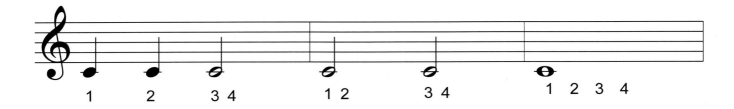

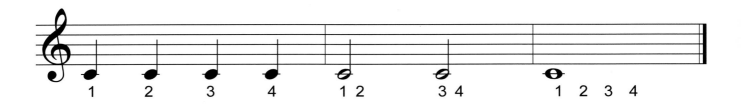

In this exercise we are counting just the timing of the quarter
notes, half notes and whole notes in the song First Melody.

Place your right hand thumb (finger #1) on middle C.
Notice that we are using only the C key in this exercise.
This is so we can focus just on the counting of the notes
without looking for other keys. Remember, with half notes
the key is held down for two counts. With whole notes the
key is down for all four counts.

The mind is very forgiving on counting mistakes when counting
silently. It is best to count out loud to catch counting mistakes.

Work towards an even count of 1,2,3,4,1,2,3,4; like marching
or counting off seconds.

First Melody finding the keys

These are the note names to First Melody. Find the proper keys.
Repeat these a few times to become familiar with their locations.

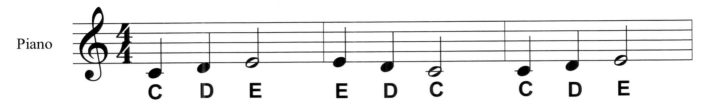

Piano

C D E   E D C   C D E

E D C   D   E   C

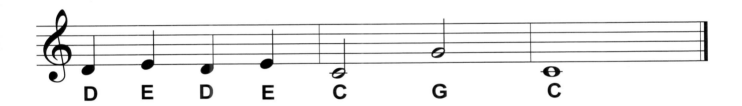

D E D E C   G   C

What to do on this page:

1. First find middle C.
   Place your right hand fingers onto the keys C,D,E,F,G.

2. Make believe each finger is glued to a key.

3. We practiced the count of this song on the previous page.
   Just play the notes of the song until they become easy to find.

First Melody final stage

Fingers 1,2,3,4,5 on keys C,D,E,F,G.

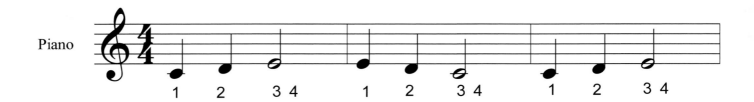

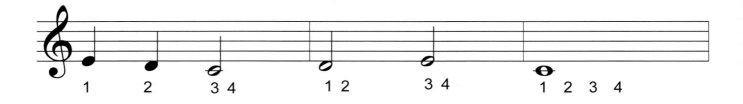

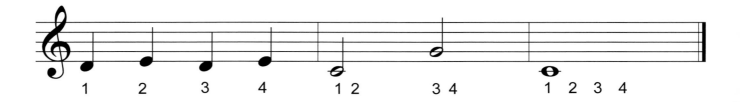

Now we put the count and proper keys together.

1. Two pages ago we started working on this song. First we worked just on counting the quarter notes, half notes and whole notes. Then, one page ago, we focused on finding the keys to be played.

2. Next we need to put these together. Count SLOW at first, out loud. First note on count 1, second note on count 2, third note on count 3 and hold that half note down through count 4. Then start again on count 1 of the next measure. It's OK to start and stop while counting and finding keys also to repeat sections until they become familiar.

3. Our goal: to fit the proper keys into a steady 1,2,3,4 count..

Five Finger counting

All the notes of this song, Five Finger, have been changed
to C so we can practice just counting. Remember our goal
is a steady 1,2,3,4 count, like counting while marching.

Five Finger finding the keys

Find middle C. Place fingers 1,2,3,4,5 on C,D,E,F,G.

On this page we focus on finding each key. No focus on counting.
Just find the keys. Become familiar with these before going on to the
following page of reading the notes and counting at the same time.

Five Finger: final stage

We combine each proper key with an even count for each measure and we have our song. Our goal is to achieve an even count with no pausing between measures, like marching to a count of four: 1,2,3,4.

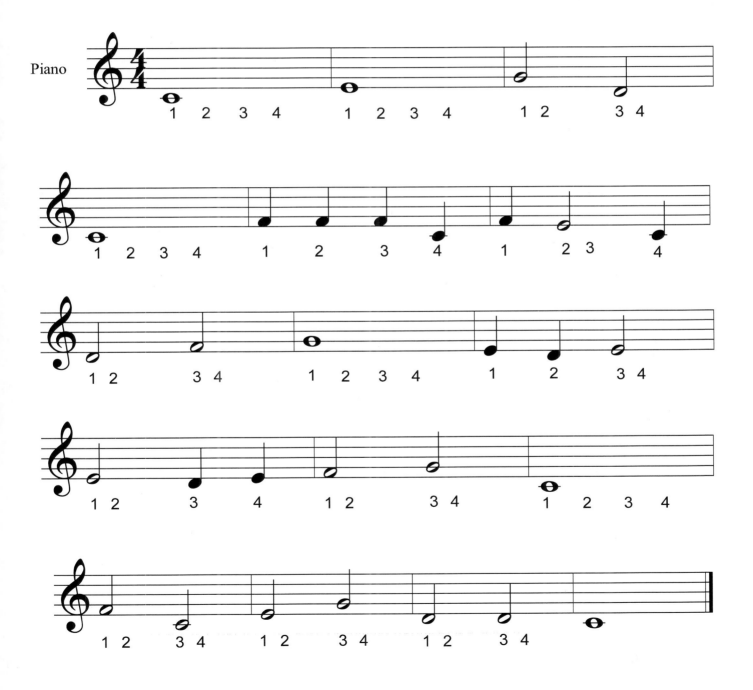

Walk in the park

Remember to count 1,2,3,4

How often should I practice? Repetition is the key to learning
any instrument. Short practices, a few times a day are good.
Remember. Rome was not built in a day.

How fast should I count? Counting is not about speed. Start counting
all new songs slowly. Strive to count steady, without stopping and starting
between measures. Once the song can be played slowly at a steady
1,2,3,4 count; then increase the counting speed if desired.

Perfection is not required and stay away from critics. Just do
our best. Most listeners don't hear the simple mistakes but they
do hear stops and starts during a song. New players always stop
and start while learning. It's just part of the process.

EZ to walk

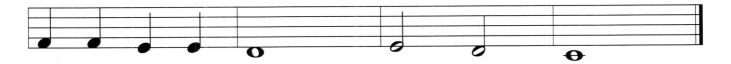

1. This song contains whole notes (4 counts), dotted half notes (3 counts), half notes (2 counts) and quarter notes (1 count). Practice counting this song by playing a single key as you did for earlier songs on pages 10 and 13 of this book.

2. Do your best to achieve a steady count of 1,2,3,4 with the single key. Start slow. We can always increase our counting speed as the timing becomes more familiar.

3. Next become familiar with the notes without the counting. Once the notes can be found easily we will be ready to begin playing the notes and counting, slowly at first, until finding each key while counting becomes familiar as a team effort of your fingers.

Five Finger Scramble

First use a single key to tap out the note values while counting 1,2,3,4.
Next focus on finding the notes of this song. Write the note
names under any that give you trouble. Once comfortable finding
the keys, add your 1,2,3,4 count. Goal: playing while counting.
Then, **playing while counting evenly.**

When do I use my left hand?

The left hand and right hand use the same counting.

The counting of the whole notes, dotted half notes, half notes and quarter notes is the same. Four counts for the whole notes, three for the dotted half notes, two for the half notes and one for quarter notes.

The **Left Hand** notes are placed in a new group of measures that sit directly below the right hand measures. The count lines up with both measures. Right and left hand measures look like these below:

This "treble clef" sign means
we are playing right hand notes.

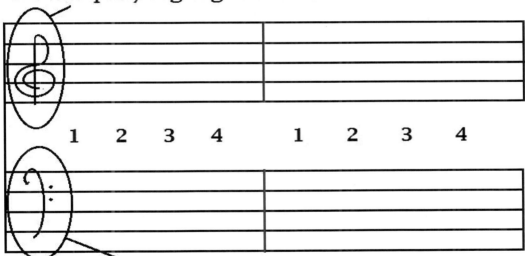

This "Bass clef" sign means left hand notes.

The placement of the left hand notes C,D,E,F,G on the left hand staff is different from the right hand note placement. Lets' explain this on the next page.

Lines and Spaces of a Staff

Our left hand notes are on different lines and spaces than those for the right hand. We will help you throughout this book to become familiar with their location on the left hand staff. As shown below **middle C** key is the midpoint between the left and right hand staffs. Our right hand thumb will always sit on middle C.

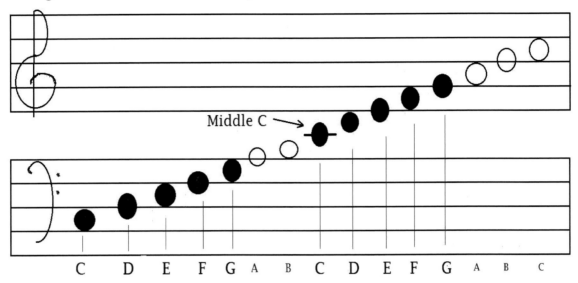

For placement of your hands let's look at the photo on page 4. As with the earlier right hand songs in this book, your right hand is placed on C,D,E,F,G; starting at **middle C**.

Your **left hand pinky finger** (finger #5), is placed on the C key located seven white keys to the left of middle C. Your remaining four fingers play keys D,E,F,G.

Things to know

Below is **a good exercise** for your ten fingers. As seen
on page 4, find middle C for your right hand. And for your left
hand find the C key seven white keys to the left of middle C.
The left hand notes show the C to G keys your left hand plays.

Play the quarter notes below going from C to G and back, first
with your 5 right hand fingers, then with your 5 left hand fingers.

The challange comes when we try playing the two hands at the
same time: two C's, two D's, two E's, etc. Getting the two groups
of fingers to cooperate will be an on going challange for you.
Do this exercise daily as a warm up.

C D E F   G F E D   C D E F   G F E D

Most teachers teach a half hour lesson once a week. Their expectation is
that the student spend some time daily working on a song, resulting in
being able to play the tune the following lesson, before going on to the
next song.

The speed of your count is up to you. Always start a new song or
exercise with a slow count of 1,2,3,4. The exercise above should first
be played slowly with the focus on pushing both right and left hand
keys down at the same time. Once your fingers are cooperating start
increasing your counting speed but keep the counting steady.

Our focus throughout these pages is on learning to read these
5 notes for each hand and becoming comfortable with counting
the timing of each note, resulting in the two hands cooperating
with each other to produce some rewarding and enjoyable results.

1st 'C' Song

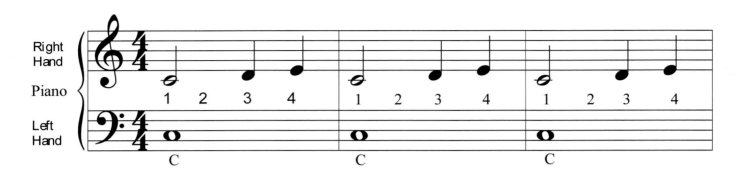

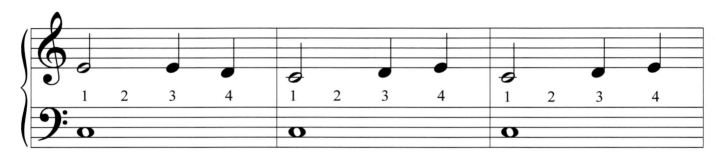

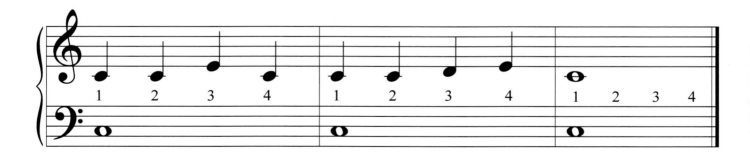

This is your first song using two hands. Follow your 1,2,3,4 count.
Both hands play a key on count 1. Use your left hand 'pinky' to
play the whole note C key in each measure. Hold it down for the
4 counts while your right hand is also playing.

In the Beginning, Bagpipes

Remember. Count out loud.

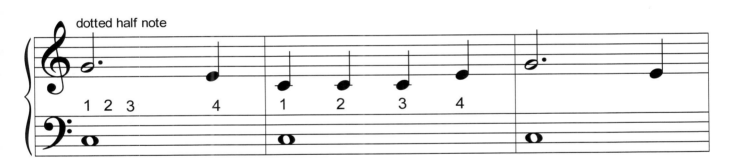

This song has mostly right hand quarter notes but watch for the
dotted half notes (3 counts). Your left hand again uses just the
C key on count one. Become familiar with the right and left hand
counting of this song by playing just a single key with each hand
as we did on pages 10 and 13 earlier.

Finger '1' is Thumb

Ist 'C' song + busier left hand

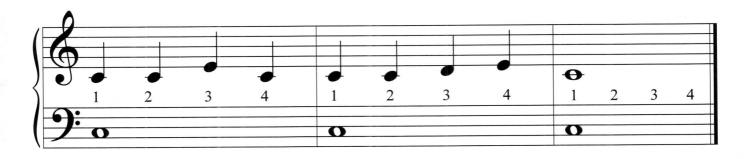

Simple Things Work

As songs get more complicated it is best to get familiar with a song by practicing each hand separately. After placing hands together work on just a few measures at a time. Counting slowly, out loud helps.

Something New: RESTS

A rest is a visual signal to **play nothing** while still counting some portion of a measure or measures of a song.

Rests are counted the way notes are counted:

 Quarter rest looks like this. It receives one count of playing nothing.

 **Half rest looks like this rectangle sitting on the middle line of the staff. Half rest receives 2 counts of silence.**

 **Whole rest looks like this, hanging from the 2nd line from the top of the staff. It means 4 counts of silence.**

Quarter rest   Whole rest   Half rest

You will see rests in most of the following songs. Just keep counting while nothing is played.

The Big Three

This song is two pages long.

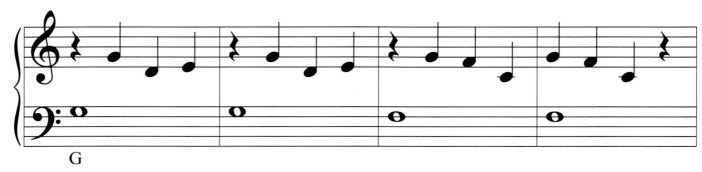

The left hand notes in this song are either C,F or G.
Again we have quarter rests, on count 1 or count 4
of the right hand. It is OK to write in note names.

The Big Three

Remember this: we do not need to play perfectly to allow ourselves
the enjoyment of our successes at the keyboard. Play your instrument
daily, if only for a few minutes. And play our earlier songs often. We want
a strong base of counting, reading notes and finding the proper keys.

The Full Monty

Watch for the quarter note rests throughout this song.

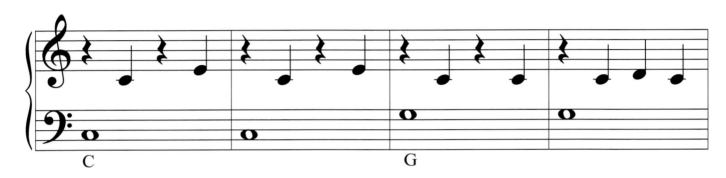

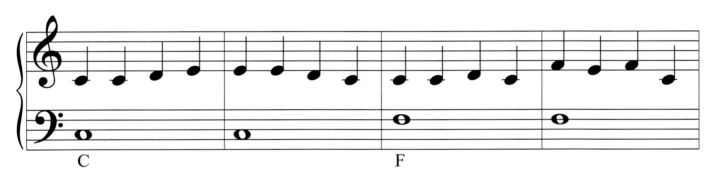

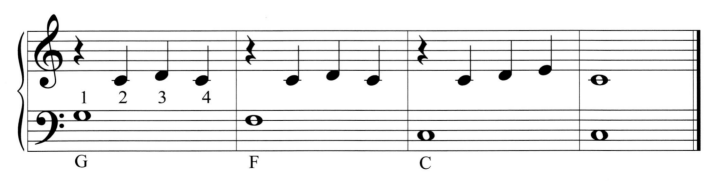

Morning Stretch

Left hand plays on count 1, then the right hand plays counts 2,3,4.

Refer to page 10 and 13. Pick a single key for each hand to play while first practicing the counting of this song. Your counting is the common link between your two hands. We can wander aimlessly along the page, guessing at what goes where or follow a count. Best to follow the count.

All Cows Eat Grass

Print the Left Hand note letters below

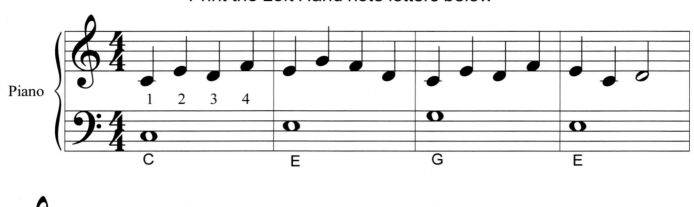

C   E   G   E

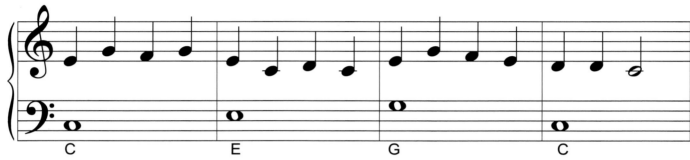

C   E   G   C

___   ___   ___   ___

___   ___   ___

Two Quarters and a Half

Rest Assured

We have a few half rests and a whole rest in this song. Remember to count.

Piano

1 2 3 4   1 2 3 4   1 2 3 4

C   E C

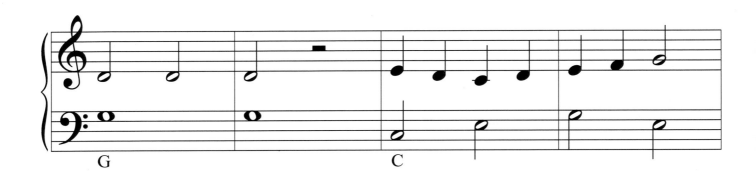

G   C

C D

A whole rest takes up 4 counts, the whole measure.
A half rest shares the measure with other notes.

Happy Daisy

Watch for the dotted half notes. Worth 3 counts.

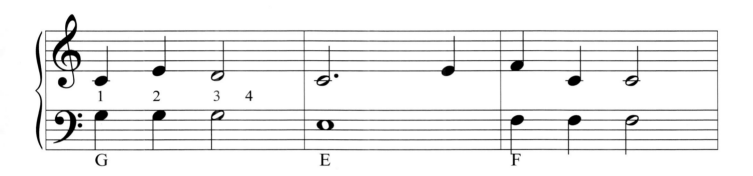

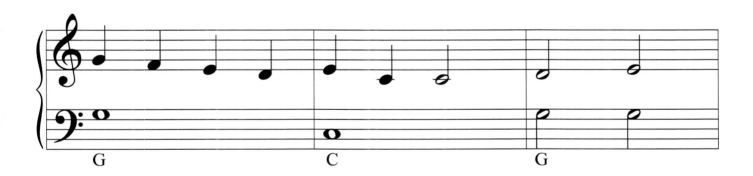

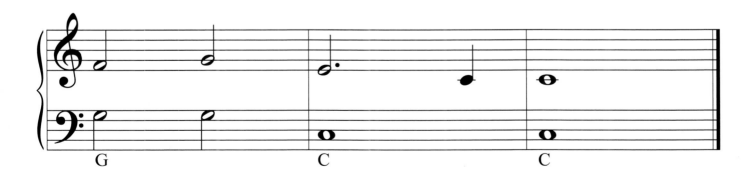

36

Walking

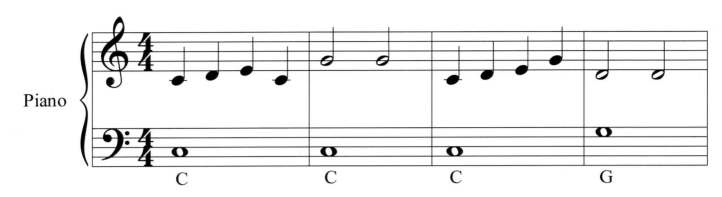

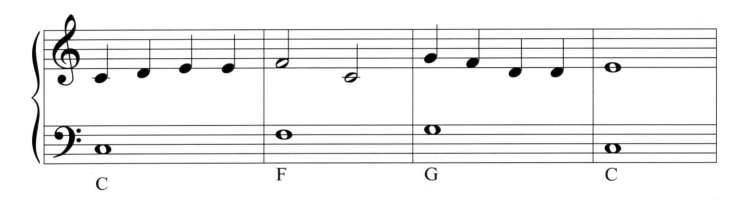

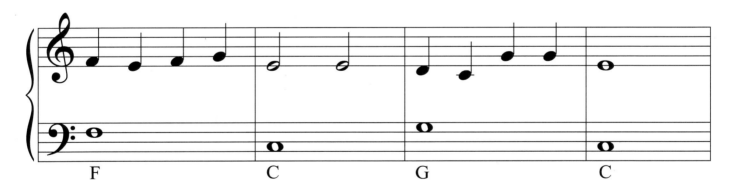

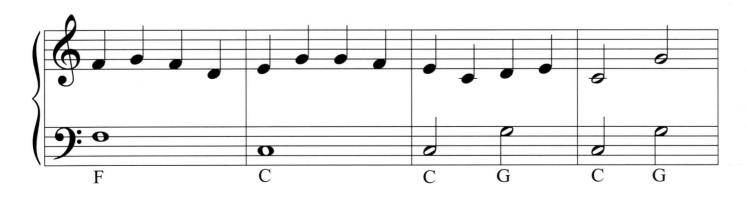

Walking

C   G

C

Partial Chords in the Left Hand

The next group of songs will have more demand on your left hand. Sometimes you will be asked to play two keys at the same time with your left hand. This is called playing **partial chords**. A **chord** is a group of keys pushed down at the same time with one hand.
This will produce a bigger sound.

Below is an example of partial chords:

1	2	3	4	1	2	3	4

The C and G are played as one.　　　The C and E are played as one.

Let's review left hand note names for a minute.

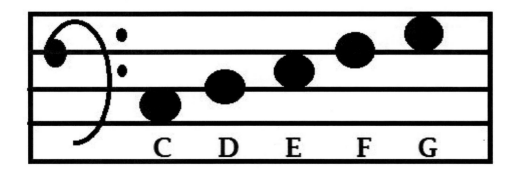

Wait for it

This song contains half note rests worth 2 counts each. On counts
1,2 the left hand plays, and on counts 3,4 the right hand plays.

40

2,3,4

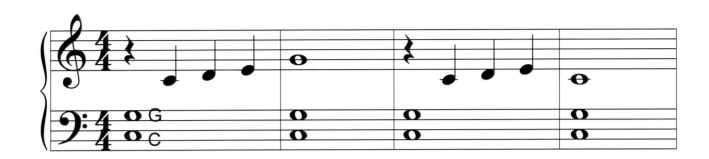

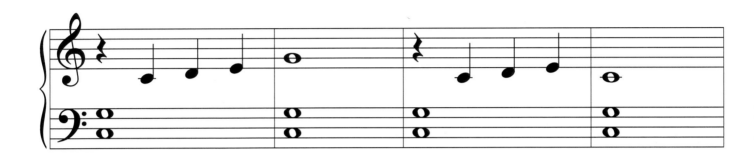

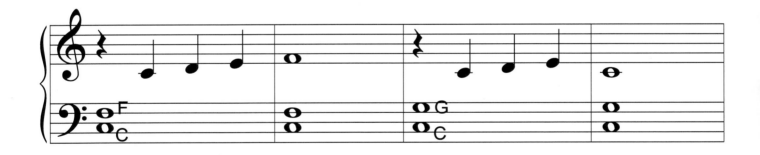

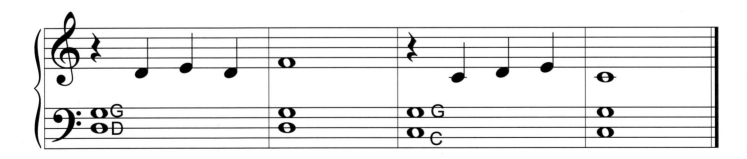

Our left hand partial chords change a few times in this song.
The chord remains the same for the first eight measures, then
changes on the ninth measure, again on measure 11, 13 and 15.
These changes have been labeled next to the notes.

Two Quarters +

We have added more left hand to the song Two Quarters and a Half.
When one left hand note is above the other, push down the two left
hand keys at the same time.

Two Quarters, a Half & More

This is a version of Two Quarters + with more left hand notes.

Piano

Practice the left hand by itself while counting out loud. Your goal is to have a steady 1,2,3,4 count with no pausing between measures to look for notes. If necessary leave your whole notes a bit early to set up your hand for the partial chord on count 1 of the next measure.

Happy Daze

Work with each hand seperately before putting hands together.
This song is full of harmony notes, like a good sounding duo.
Count slowly at first.

The Waltz

Up to now we have been counting 1,2,3,4 for each measure of music. There is a type of song with a count of 1,2,3. It is the waltz. The waltz has been around forever and is still a popular dance.

A song with 3 counts in a measure is easily identified by looking at the first measure of the song. There are two large numbers, one above the other. The top number tells how many counts are in each measure of the song. See the two examples below. One shows 3 counts per measure, the other shows 4.

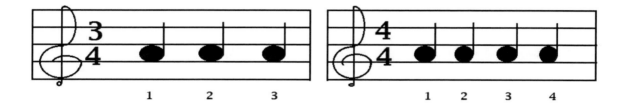

Each measure of a waltz contains just three counts, so no room for any whole notes (4 counts). The largest note to fit in a waltz measure is the dotted half note, receiving 3 counts. The songs in this next group are waltzes. Enjoy.

Quick Review

Our hand positions will continue to be
the same throughout this book:

C,D,E,F,G   **Middle C,D,E,F,G**
Left hand   *Right hand*

Remember: Thumbs are #1.

Any rests in these Waltz songs will be half or quarter rests.

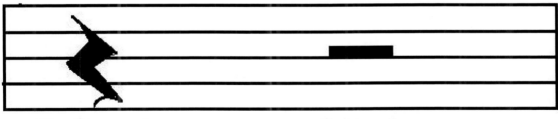

Quarter rest   **Half rest**
1 count .   **2 counts**

Astaire Waltz

Any left hand notes giving you a problem? Write those in under the note.

Finale

This song follows a left hand pattern. Left hand counts 2 and 3 are all
G notes. Just focus on the notes located on count 1 of both hands.
Soon you can just follow the right hand notes to play this song because
you'll know that counts 2 and 3 are always the G key.

Stuffenough 3

Remember, an even count of 1,2,3 for each measure is our goal.
We tend to want to pause after each measure, like counting
1,2,3,pause, 1,2,3, pause, 1,2,3, pause. Try not to pause
between each measure. We need a steady 1,2,3,1,2,3,1,2,3.

Stuffenough 3

Stay With Me

Remember. This is a waltz. Three counts to each measure.
You will enounter some half note rests (2 counts) on the
2nd page of this song.

Stay with me

The Ladder

The Ladder

More To Come

Piano

Back to beginning

See the dark vertical line with dots at the beginning of this song.
This is a repeat sign. Look ahead eight measures into the song
to find the mirror image of the first measure's dotted vertical lines.
At this spot, eight measures into the song, jump back to the
beginning of the song and repeat those eight measures.
Then continue to the end of the song.

More To Come Still

Here is the same song with some left hand partial chords.
Each partial chord contains a G key. These two pages can
be played as one song.

Stay With Me Too

This is a more advanced version of Stay With Me. The left hand plays a partial chord on count 1 of each measure.

Stay with me too

Call Me 'Fingers' Also

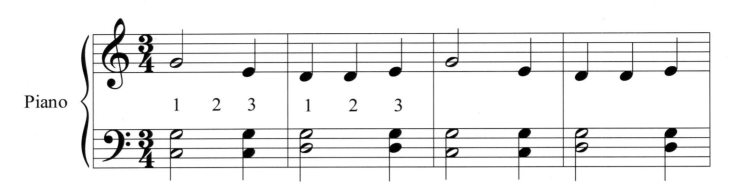

Piano